Dialogue with the Goddess

Journey into the Presence of the Goddess

Deb,
may the Goddess bless every-
thing you cook and do!
And give you rest and quiet!
Cynthia

Cynthia Lea Tootle

Copyright © 2012 Cynthia Lea Tootle

All rights reserved. No part of this book may be used, reproduced, scanned, or distributed in any manner whatsoever, without written permission from the author, except in the case of brief quotations embodied in critical articles and reviews.

Art by Alice Simms of artforthepeople.org

Cover photograph by Cynthia Lea Tootle

Cover type by Sharon (Wren) Rogers

Contact the Author at cynthia.tootle@facebook.com

Or at Reverend Tootle, 756 Silver Spring Ave, Silver Spring, MD 20910

ISBN-13: 978-1477501177

ISBN-10: 1477501177

Printed in the United States of America

Acknowledgments

I must start by thanking my dear friend Rev Jane Batt who has encouraged me to write a book for years. With spiritual guidance and practically nudging, Jane pushed me over the resistance and into doing. Greater love has no woman than a friend who helps with the boring stuff in order to allow the good stuff to happen.

Ellyn Dye told me to write whole new sections of the book and gave me practical advice on how to publish for which I am very grateful

My thanks to Donna Zagar, Deborah Thomas, and the other wonderful women of the Takoma Park Chapel who read early versions of the book and encouraged me to persist.

My thanks to Linda Mason who is a good neighbor and excellent proof reader.

My thanks to the exceptional healer and friend Rev Mardi Fisher without whom I doubt I would be alive today and the person I am.

And thanks to anyone who chooses to make this journey to the Goddess with me.

I am the Ancient Mother. I am the source of all creation. You are my perfect, beloved Child. There is nothing in the universe I love more than you. You may have forgotten me but I have never for a moment forgotten you. You are in my arms now and for all eternity.

                        Message Channeled by the Author

Contents

Preface	1
Prayers to the Mother Goddess	3
Prayers to the Goddess of 10,000 Names	17
Prayers of the Dark Days	51
Everyday Prayers	65
Prayers for Special Occasions	75
Begin your own Dialogue with the Goddess	85
Hearing the Goddess	91
On the Path to the Goddess	99
Index of Goddesses	111
About the Author	113

Preface

On a beautiful spring evening, under a clear starlit sky and a giant full moon, a small group of women met in the park by Greenbelt Lake. We wore long dresses and our best jewelry. We brought blankets, food, candles, crystals, and our hopeful imaginations. We were a consciousness raising group of women of different ages, different lifestyles, and different religions. We were trying to find some way that was true to our feminine selves to worship God. We had little knowledge of the Goddess—as little was available in 1979—so we took what bits we could find and embroidered them with our enthusiasm and hope and created ceremony. We danced and sang and giggled. We were embarrassed and thrilled.

As I look back now, after decades of study and ceremony, I know that the Goddess was delighted to dance with us that starlit night.

And She has led me ever since.

I didn't start out my life knowing the Goddess. I was raised in the Roman Catholic Church with saints being tortured to death in every window of our little church. God was male and his Son was male and the Holy Ghost probably was too. Mary, the mother of God and the Queen of Heaven, we were carefully taught, was NOT GOD and must not be worshiped under the pain of mortal sin and everlasting hell.

I was raised in the 1950's when expectations for a person were very much dependent on gender. I was called "little mom" and was expected to help my housewife mother take care of my three brothers and the house. But I inherited my father's gift of mind. So I found myself as a studious, book-loving teenager in the 1960's preparing myself to go to college to be an engineer like my father while trying to survive my mother's expectation for a popular daughter.

I graduated college and got a job as an engineer. I struggled to handle the prejudices and expectations of my coworkers-and life in general—with the constant backdrop of the Vietnam Conflict. My older brother volunteered and served in the US Army in Vietnam and Thailand.

Preface

My younger brother received a draft notice each June and planned his trip to Canada when he graduated. In January 1973, I was on a long business trip. I heard the news that the military draft had been ended but had little time to be happy that my younger brother would not be forced to choose between his country and a war in which he did not believe. I went to a little Roman Catholic Church near my apartment that Sunday when I got home ready to thank God for this deliverance.

The sermon that day was given by the assistant pastor. He was totally unhappy with the US government and could not see how we could support it—because the Supreme Court had ruled in Roe vs. Wade. As I sat in the audience and listened to him rant, I became very clear. No matter how much I prayed, how spiritual I became, how holy and devoted, I would never have a voice in this place. I did not believe what he said and I could not support the institution that gave him a platform and expected me to be silent. I walked out of the church that day and never went back.

I didn't replace this religion and its practices with another. I didn't even look for another church of which to be part for 20 years. I found my spiritual life in women's circles. I found mystical experiences with psychics and shamans.

And eventually I learned to approach and open to the Goddess directly.

I have been guided by Her to pass on some of my experiences so it might be easier for others who might seek the Goddess. I open myself to serve Her; I put my trust in Her that She will guide me as to how to serve you.

So mote it be.

Cynthia

Prayers to the Mother Goddess

Many religions and traditions, ancient and modern, worship the Divine in Feminine form. The Ancient Mother is the oldest and most powerful representation of the Divine Feminine. The figures of the Goddess date back over 25,000 years and are found around the world. She represents the basic life-giving principle. She is immense and complex and every representation of Her enriches our understanding of the Divine.

When I want to reach past the limitations of cultures and religions to the Divine, I pray to the Mother Goddess. Here are prayers and poems that have come to me when I turned to Her.

We Ask Your Blessing

Ancient Mother, Source of all Creation, we open ourselves to you. We implore you to use us as a channel of your pure love and healing energy. Bless all aspects of our humanness with your compassion and acceptance that we might love and accept ourselves. Bless all the dark aspects of ourselves and help us to own them and eliminate all need for drama here today. Bless every hurtful word that we have said and hurtful act that we have done until we understand forgiveness. Bless and magnify all that is sacred within us until we understand that all that is within us is sacred.

Amen

The Our Mother

Ancient Mother, who is in our hearts and everywhere, we honor Your many names. We willingly open our beings to Your loving energy that Your will be done on earth. Give us this day a luscious abundance and bless us with Your unconditional love as we practice loving one another. Lead us always into the temptation of Your glorious Presence and deliver us from all separation. For Thine is the power and glory within us all, forever and ever.

Amen

The Mother Goddess

Mother Goddess Invocation

Goddesses Ancient and Living,
We welcome you into our lives today.
Fill this place with your brightness
And your shadows.

Illuminate our hearts
With transforming love,
That we might see and love
All the parts of our Selves.

Radiate your Love
Into all our dark corners.
Let your light show us
Who we truly are.

Let rain fall upon us soon
To bless us with forgiveness
And cleanse us of anger and separateness.
Let us rest in the moist soil as seeds,
Full of potential.

Goddesses Ancient and Living
We ask You to help us grow
Until we are as blessed as the flowers,
Whose roots are nurtured in your dark soil
And whose faces are always turned to You.

Winter Full Moon Prayer

Queen of the Heavens,
Bless us, your children, this sacred night,
Bless us with the sense of your Divine Presence.

O, Ancient Mother,
May we know on this long night of Winter
That the darkness is not a sign you have deserted us
But that we rest and grow in your Holy Womb.
On this sacred night,
Keep us in safety and lead us to wonder.
Let your darkness fill us with peace,
Let your shining stars fill us with joy,
Let your glowing moon fill us to overflowing with your love.

Magnificent Goddess of the Night,
Bless us, your children,
With a new year more wonderful than we can imagine.
May we be happy
May we be successful
May we be kind
May we grow
May we live
May we love
May we rest each night with joy and peace in your arms.
So mote it be.

Spring Full Moon Prayer

This blessed spring,
This sacred night,
Smiling Mother,
Hear our sighs.

The sweet perfume
Of the evening breeze
Smells of your love,
Flowers and earth.

Shining Mother
Of this gentle night,
Bless the tender shoots
Of new beginnings.

We dance with you,
Our sweet Mother,
And sing of life
And childhood found.

Summer Full Moon Prayer

We wake in the night
Called by your silver light
To dance with bare feet
On your cool earth
With our arms and shadows
Reaching for you.

How blessed the cool dark of night,
After the blinding heat of the summer day.

Thank you, Mother, for beaming on us.

The gift of your gentle light
Moves us to sing
Moves us to dance
Moves us to dream
Moves us to you.

How blessed are we, your lost children,
We have found you again in our sky.

Missing You

The Sun holds sway
These hot summer days.
The old oak gifts us
precious shade in living patterns
of shadow and light.
We thank the old oak
For the gift of beauty and relief.
But we miss the softer Moon
Hidden overhead
By branches that seem too solid
In the sacred night.
Oh, we love the fruits
Of summer:
The growth and movement
Of plants and birds and bugs.
We thank the Sun
For these gifts
Of beauty and abundance.
But we miss the mother Moon
Hidden overhead.

Goddess of the Sun Benediction

Goddess of the Sun,
We thank You, with full hearts,
For Your Presence here among us today.
We thank You
For the healing we have experienced
For the forgiveness
For the prosperity
For the rest
For the light
And most especially, we thank You
For the love we have experienced today.
We ask You, oh Goddess of the Sun,
To bless us as we leave this place.
Shine gently down on us
And allow the rain we need to come.

Today in Joy and Wonder

Sweet Mother,

I know today that I am Your perfect child.

All my heart is filled with love.

I live today in joy and wonder at the world You have created.

I smell the roses.

Thank You, Mother, for creating something so perfectly beautiful to see and smell.

I see the sky and clouds.

Thank You, Mother, for creating such drama and dynamic beauty to bless us every day.

I walk in the shade of the trees.

Thank You, Mother, for creating living beings of such variety and dignity and color to share our lives.

I feel the people here.

Thank You, Mother, for being present in the world around me, in their eyes, in their faces, and in their hearts.

I know today that I am Your perfect child.

All my heart is filled with love.

I live today in joy and wonder at the world You have created.

Amen

Ancient Mother Invocation

We call upon You, Ancient Mother, by all Your many names. We ask You to be here with us today. We ask You, we invite You, we beg. We demand Your presence as a squawking infant demands its Mother.

We acknowledge our position as Your beloved Children. We call to You, Ancient Mother of all beings, with utter confidence that You hear our prayer and answer.

We open ourselves to Your Presence and Power. Prepare us this evening to be Your channel to transform this planet.

Amen

The Prayer Bertha Requested

In the soft air around me, I feel your loving presence, Goddess Mother, surrounding me.

In the shifting light of spring as clouds and leaves dance in the air, I feel the constant light of your presence, Goddess Mother, in my eyes.

Smelling the sweet scent of spring flowers, I feel your presence, Goddess Mother, within.

And I am filled with love and joy today.

Thank you, Goddess Mother.

Amen

A Prayer for the Soul's Healing

Ancient Mother,
who created me,
is there room for peace
in my busy mind?

I am willing
if not yet able,
to let go
of my story
of my history
of my justifications.

I surrender today
to your story for me,
Ancient Mother.

If I start today
being your precious child,
can you heal
all the scars
all the broken places
that I can't even see?

I choose today
to surrender.

I choose today
to believe.

Help me,
Ancient Mother.

Prayers to the Goddess of 10,000 Names

Many people over the eons have described beings who embody the Divine Feminine. They have created images, stories, and names. Some of these Goddesses we only know by images left behind. We know a great deal about other Goddesses and how the devotees saw and knew of Her. Some Goddesses are still worshiped today.

When I studied these Goddesses I became aware of Divinity in new ways. One Goddess would embody infinite compassion. Another Goddess teaches the immense power of the Divine to create and destroy the people and planet. Another Goddess would portray the gentle qualities of comfort and protection. Another Goddess shows us the awesome power of fierce protection against all comers. Another Goddess has lessons on the breadth of perspective of the Divine to see beyond the truncated stories of our lives on this earthly plane. My mind cannot encompass this all at once and so each story helps me open up a little more.

I offer you some prayers to Goddesses who have touched me.

The Maiden

Sweet, swift, graceful Maiden,
Full of energy and magic,
Be with us now.

Bless this new beginning
And all the new beginnings
In our lives.

Hunt the beast
Ride the horse
And take us with you.

Love the youth
And make him glad
To be in our arms.

Dance with abandon
Sing with joy
As we join your ecstasy.

Sweet Maiden
Beloved Sister
Welcome to our circle.

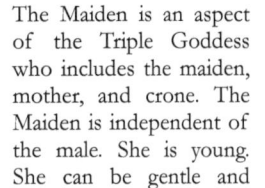

The Maiden is an aspect of the Triple Goddess who includes the maiden, mother, and crone. The Maiden is independent of the male. She is young. She can be gentle and nurturing or a fierce warrior or hunter.

Crone Invocation

Old lady, hag, crone
we call you forth!
from behind the facade
of ugly, helpless, dimwitted,
beyond the jokes and disdain,
we call you forth!

From silly portrayals of
warts, wrinkles, stink
bag ladies in alleys
crazy ladies in nursing homes
we call you forth!

Old lady, hag, crone
we call you forth!
that we might see in you
what divinity is there
wisdom of the ages
strength which has been tested
compassion that knows from experience
love of self that flows to all
silence beyond words

Goddess Crone
we call you forth!

The Crone aspect of the Triple Goddess is much derided in our culture. This Goddess is an old woman wise from years of experience and observation. She is the midwife and healer. She can see beyond the present time and place. It was a joy to find Her power in the ancient worship of the Crone.

Hear Me, Lady Kwan Yin

Compassionate One, whose name says it all, She who hears the cries of the world, I am humbled by the breadth of your love.

When Your compassion blesses the abusers, the perpetrators, the worst as only the Divine can or would, I know there is compassion for my arrogance of self-importance, my dark secrets, and shames. I ask for your compassion.

Sweet Lady, you ride the mighty dragons above the crashing ocean waves without losing your serenity and stillness. I dare ask that you let me rest in your stillness when the waves of my life crash around me.

Kwan Yin, you promised to remain until all creatures can pass to nirvana with you. My eyes fill with tears knowing my small, imperfect self will not be abandoned. When I reach Nirvana, I will look over my shoulder and find you there.

In your name, Kwan Yin, I offer all the compassion and love my humble heart can hold to those beside me in this world.

Kwan Yin is a Buddhist Bodhisattva from China. A Bodhisattva is a human who has reached enlightenment and could move on to Nirvana but She vowed to not leave until all of us have gone before her. Her name means 'She who hears the cries of the world.' She is the Goddess of Compassion and the Goddess Who Takes Away Fear. Statues and paintings often show Her holding a vessel which contains the dew of heaven.

Lady Kwan Yin

Shakti Invocation

Dancing Goddess
With spine aflame
From root to exploding crown,
We daringly whisper
Your glowing name,
Shakti, Shakti, Shakti.

Dance with us,
Your mortal daughters,
Light our bodies
Till we burn all doubt
And joyously explode with you,
Shakti, Shakti, Shakti.

Now we dance,
Goddesses and women,
Opening our arms and hearts
To Gods and men,
That we may spin in perfect balance,
Shakti, Shakti, Shakti.

In Hinduism, Shakti is the Divine Feminine that is the universal principle of energy, power, and creativity. Each male god is paired with an incarnation of her in order to activate and manifest his potential.

Prayer to Gaia

Our hearts and minds are full of You, Gaia-Mother. No words of gratitude are enough to thank you for all the gifts you have given to us. This night we acknowledge that every plant, animal, fish, and bird is a child of our marvelous Mother, Gaia. The water in us flows in rhythm with the oceans, streams, rains, lakes—the waters of Our Mother. The air in our lungs also flows in the bodies of the foxes, bears, dolphins, lions, rabbits, whales, rats, chipmunks, and circulates in the tornadoes and hurricanes. We thank You, Gaia, for we are a small part of Your magnificent whole.

Blessed Be.

> Gaia is the Goddess that embodies the planet Earth itself. Recently this name has been associated with the awareness of the planet as a living entity.

Invocation of the Goddess Flora

Sweet Flora,
As children
We worship you
by climbing your trees
picking your weed-flowers
planting your miraculous seeds.
As adults
We worship you
by planting your fields
tending your flower beds
mowing your grass.
As elders
We worship you
by luxuriating in your gardens
contemplating your blossoms
smelling your roses.

Sweet Flora
We ask you tonight
to walk on our planet
spreading life.
We ask you tonight
to walk on our continent.
We ask you tonight
to walk on our country.
We ask you tonight
to walk on the streets of our town.

The ancient Romans worshiped the Goddess Flora in the spring as the Goddess of flowering plants. You can see where She has passed by the flowers blooming in Her wake.

Sweet Flora,
We might drink to Bacchus
We might lust after Venus or Apollo
We might fear Jupiter or Mars
But we love you, Flora.
each delicate flower
each tree
each vine
each herb
How could we not love you?

Sweet Flora
I ask you tonight
to walk on my street
I ask you tonight
to walk in my garden.
I ask you tonight
to walk in my home.
I ask you tonight
to walk in my body.
I ask you tonight
to walk in my mind.
I ask you tonight
to walk in my heart.

Sweet Flora,
We ask you tonight
to walk
here.

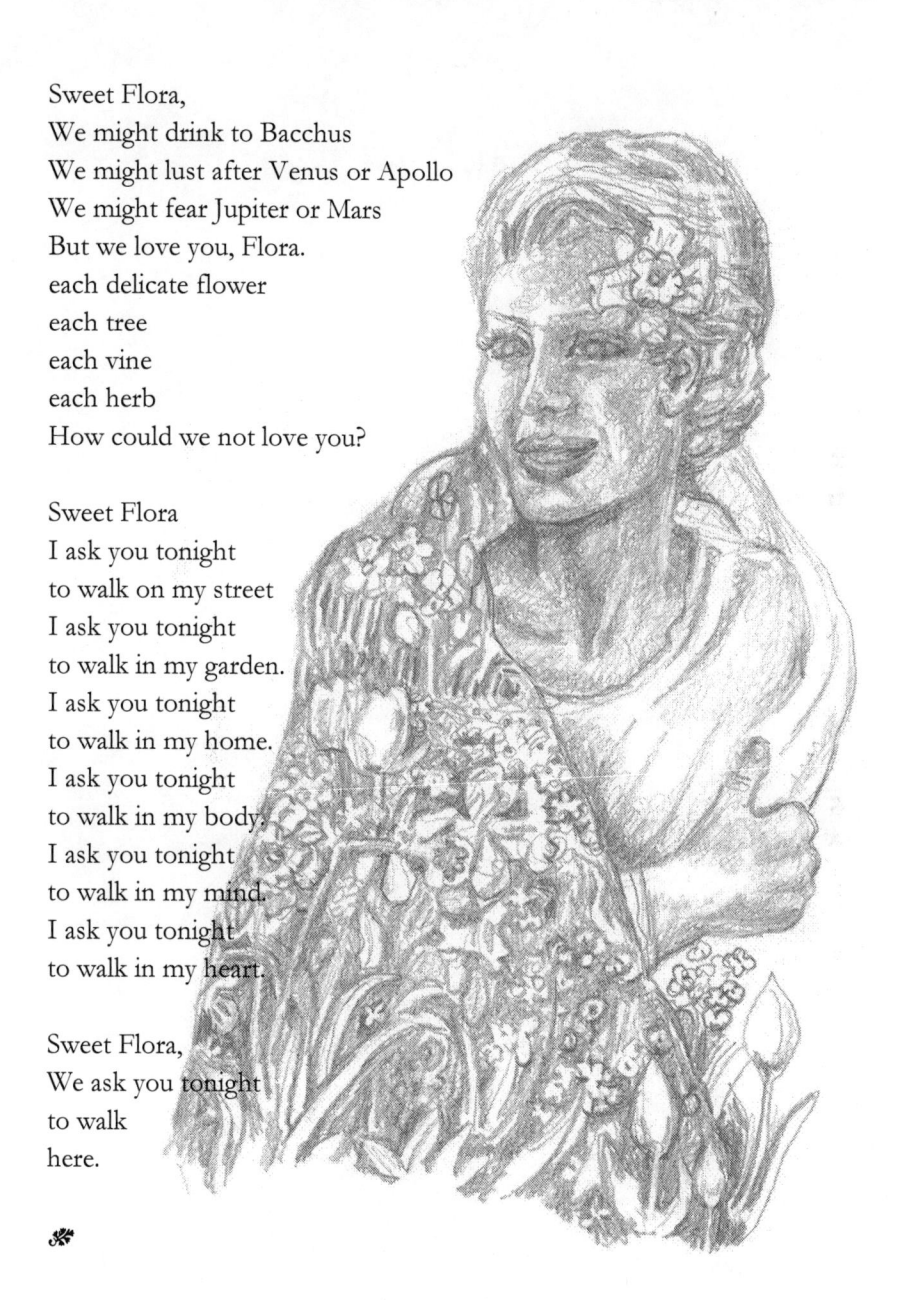

Call to Durga

Durga, Durga, Durga
You promised to come when the demons
of lust, greed, and ego are winning.
Now, the demons of lust, greed,
and ego are making a mess.
The waters are polluted.
The air is thick with toxins.
The soil is depleted.
The creatures of sea, air,
and ground are dying.
Our hearts and souls are clouded
by hurt and ego.
You promised to come!
We call You.
Durga, Durga, Durga

Durga is the powerful mother Goddess of Hinduism. She rides a tiger and slays the demons of lust, greed, and ignorance. She brought forth an army of women from Her womb and Kali from Her head to battle monsters.

An Act of Faith

I am peaceful tonight

Though much seems grim.

I am peaceful tonight

Though yesterday's troubles seem to still be here.

I am peaceful tonight

Though I cannot perceive the change.

I am peaceful tonight

Because I have called Durga

I am peaceful tonight

Because She promised to come.

I am peaceful tonight.

When Durga finished conquering the demons, and monsters the gods asked that She stay and rule the world. She declined but as She left. She promised to return when we call her.

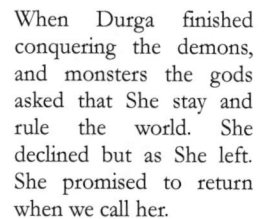

Willendorf Goddess

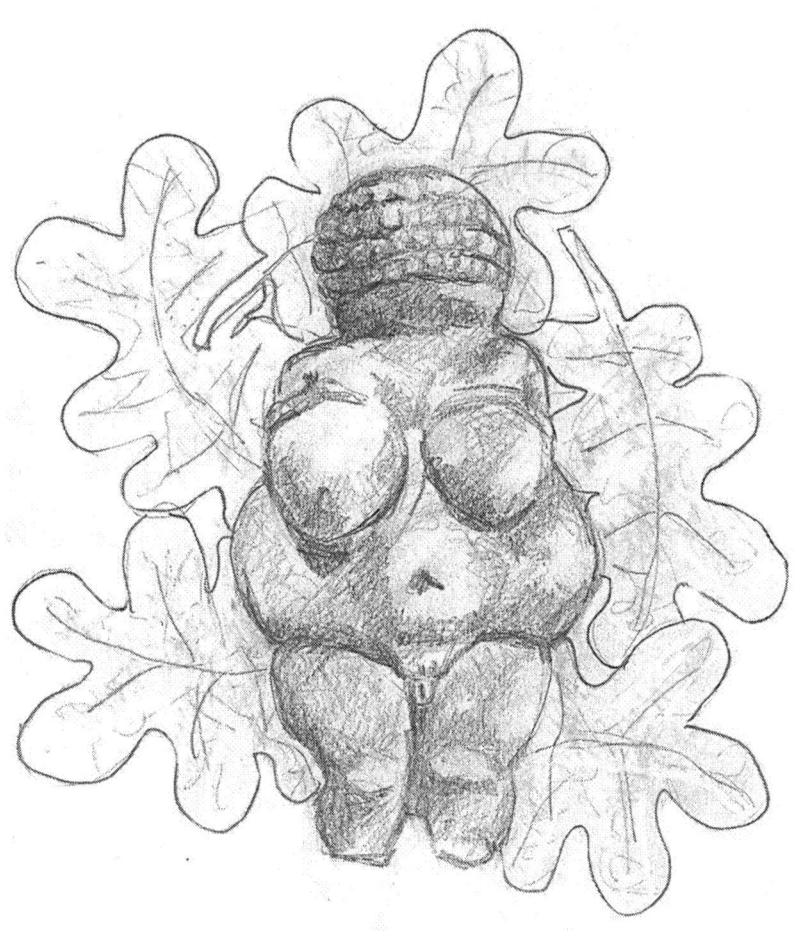

Ancient Goddess
with lavish breasts
rounded belly
naked sex
abundant thighs

How lovingly created
so long ago

I feel humble
before your image
like the artist
who did not dare
to form your face

What would be
in your eyes
if they could see
what I see in the mirror
lavish breasts
rounded belly
naked sex
abundant thighs
I am formed in your image

No matter how
scholars belittle you
You are clearly
the god that created me

No matter how
our culture
criticizes this shape,

I am in the image
of Divinity

I am yours, Mother.

All we know of the Venus of Willendorf is a statue estimated to be 25,000 years old. It is one of many small statues found in Europe that portrays the mother goddesses of ancient times.

Amaterasu's Prayer

I'm in the dark
the cave of depression
the cave of fear
I hear them call me out
to light their world
when mine is dark
when mine is hopeless

I hear drumming
bang bang thump thump bang
snickers
laughter
roars
What has made the gods so happy?

Uzume, You outrageous slut!
How can You be so bold?
How can You be so silly?

Please, Uzume, teach me how.

Amaterasu is the ancient Japanese Goddess of the Sun. After fighting with her brothers she hid herself in a cave. No matter what the gods did to entice her out she would not leave the darkness of her fear or despair. The gods then turned to the Goddess Uzume for help.

Amaterasu's Gratitude

Uzume,
Thank You for the drumming
Thank You for the laughter
Thank You for the silliness
Thank You for the outrageousness
Thank You for baring it all

Thank You for being out there
Thank You for not entering the darkness
Thank You for not asking me to shine

And thanks for getting me out of that damn cave!

In ancient Japan, Uzume was called the 'Most Alarming Female in Heaven'. When the gods could not get the Sun Goddess Amaterasu out of Her cave they called Uzume. She turned over a barrel and got up on it making noise and singing and baring Her breasts and body. She was so funny and outrageous the gods started laughing and Amaterasu came out to see what all the noise was.

Oshun

Your sweet waters flow gently
with melodic ripples
gathering strength
carving land and rock
amassing power and size
forming lakes
sweetening oceans.
I pray, Oshun, that You help me flow
as gently and with such power.

You raise the mirror
and lovingly examine Your
jewels, make-up, hairdo, clothes
admiring the womanly beauty displayed.
I pray, Oshun, that You help me
lovingly examine my image and
admire my womanly beauty.

Oshun is the Yoruban and Caribbean Orishi of sweet waters and self-adornment. An Orishi is an energy pattern that can be assumed by a person through ceremony and rituals. Worship of this Orishi survived the capture and slavery of her people.

Goddess and Saint Bridget

Spark the flame within me,
Bridget, Lady of the Smithy,
Hammer my being into a useful shape,
Temper me into strength,
Sharpen me to the point,
Wield me as You will.

Wrap me in Your blue mantle,
St. Bridget, Lady of the Mantle,
Hold me in your warm arms,
Sing me the most beautiful lullaby,
Feed the holy child,
Let the mother rest
And me be safe without her.

Lady of contradictions,
Pray understand all of me
And give me what I most need now.
Amen

In Ireland. as Goddess and Saint, Bridget has been the patron of smiths and midwives. She is a wonderful example of how the energy of the Divine Feminine lives within the religions that try to deny her.

Greeting

Greetings Serqet, blessed mother of breath!

Come fill our lungs with joy and allow us to live, love, and sing in safety.

Serpents need not be feared with You near us, Serqet. They cannot lead us astray or poison our lives or bodies when You open your arms to protect us.

In this sacred moment, we feel the breath fill our throats. We feel the air move into and out of our bodies. We know, with our total beings, the awesomeness of this act and, thank You, Great Goddess for this most precious gift.

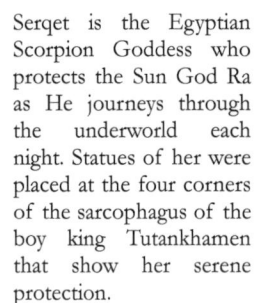

> Serqet is the Egyptian Scorpion Goddess who protects the Sun God Ra as He journeys through the underworld each night. Statues of her were placed at the four corners of the sarcophagus of the boy king Tutankhamen that show her serene protection.

Deep Breath

We take a deep breath, Serqet, in honor of You and Your power to protect. With Your blessed breath in our lungs we ask for Your protection of all the children of the Earth. Guard them from any and all poison that may come near them. Guard the women and the men who love the children. And guard all who tread dark paths this night while they journey to the light.

Amen

Green Tara

Healer Tara
I sit in your presence
allowing your image to wash over me
through me.

I feel your sweet energy, in my body, in my cells

You pour energy into me with Your right hand.
You acknowledge me with the tilt of Your head.
You see me, past, present, and future, with your seven eyes.

Thank You, Goddess,
for I know I am
healed now.

Any lingering pains are
but the illusions I choose
in this earthly life.

I know health and bliss
in your presence.

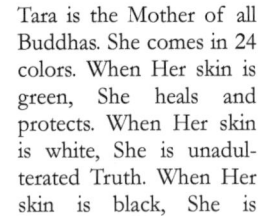

❀

Tara is the Mother of all Buddhas. She comes in 24 colors. When Her skin is green, She heals and protects. When Her skin is white, She is unadulterated Truth. When Her skin is black, She is power.

Heal Our Planet, Lady Tara

Lady Tara
Heal our planet
Bring peace to each nation
Bring peace to each religion
Bring peace to each heart

Lady Tara
Heal our planet
Feed each nation
Feed each belly
Feed each heart.

Lady Tara
Heal our planet
Protect each nation
Protect each child
Protect each heart.

Lady Tara
Heal our planet
May the air be pure air
May the water be pure water
May each heart be pure love.

Lady Tara
Heal selfish me
Bring peace to my heart
Food to my belly
Pure air to my lungs
Pure water to my lips
Pure love to my heart.

Diana

Shining Maiden,
gleaming in the clear night sky
awakening us from our sleep
to dance for you
in the cool, clean air,
we greet you with joy!

White, gray Sister
solitary and single in the sky
surrounded by life in the forest
thank you for protecting
the furred and feathered ones
from all harm.

We open the door to our hearts-
see that our hearts are not cages
but comfortable nooks
of shelter for the small
wild things you love.

Wild Goddess
join us in this circle of women
if you will
to teach us
to protect us
to share your cool perspective
to let us smell the scent
of freedom
and of wild things.

Freely come, freely go
so mote it be

Diana is the ancient Roman Goddess of the Moon. She was a huntress and the protector of wild creatures and places. She symbolized the cycles of nature and was the protector of women and children. The Romans brought her to the Celtics who adopted her as the Queen of the witches.

Nu Kua's Blessing

In this time of chaos
we ask for joy in confusion.
In this time of change
we ask for fun in messiness.

Nu Kua and Fu Hsi, grant us blessings!

In this time of collapse
we ask for joy in opportunity.
In this time of beginning
we ask for support in our labor.

Nu Kua and Fu Hsi, grant us blessings!

Nu Kua and Fu Hsi, grant us blessings!

In ancient China Nu Kua, the Divine Mother, set the cosmos spinning in orderly motion by entwining Her tail with Her husband Fu Hsi's tail.

Teach Me

White Buffalo Calf Woman, you came so long ago to the people of Turtle Island and taught them how to live and gave them the seven sacred ceremonies.

When you left the people, you left them with a promise, a prophecy: the white buffalo calf would be born to alert us to the coming of the time of peace.

The white buffalo calves have been seen. Thank you.

Although my skin is white, not red, my parents and grandparents were born on Turtle Island. I live on the land of my ancestors. I ask you, White Buffalo Calf Woman, to let me live to see the rest of the prophecy. Teach me to live in the time of peace.

Ho!

The Lakota of North America tell of the White Buffalo Calf Woman who came to the people and taught them how to live. She taught them practical skills like raising corn but also gave them powerful spiritual rituals including the vision quest, peace pipe, and sweat lodge. The Lakota do not have a concept of Goddess but consider her an ancestor.

Cerridwen

Witchy Goddess, stir the cauldron of dreams and magic.
Brew me a tonic of health and creativity.
Add love to the mix—and joy.
Add friendship and sisterhood.

I will dance with You, Cerridwen, all night around the fire
as You brew the future in Your pot.
I will pray to You
with sky-clad body
and dusty feet
and laugh at the shining moon.

Watch me with mystery in your eyes
as I, Your daughter, dance for You!

So mote it be!

Cerridwen is an ancient Celtic Goddess who stirred the cauldron of prophecy and magic. She spent a whole year brewing a potion to give Her son special powers.

Invocation of Ereshkigal

from the pure blue sky
from the golden fields of grain
from the rich dark soil
from all your elements
we call you forth
Ereshkigal

your vast perspective
your simple, complete nourishment
your quiet dark acceptance
of all that we are
we call you forth
Ereshkigal

chop off our heads
pluck off our feathers
hang us by our feet
on the day we are yours
Ereshkigal

In ancient Mesopotamia, Ereshkigal was a Grain Goddess that became the Goddess of the Underworld. She is mainly known for her role in the story of her sister Inanna who journeyed into the underworld to rescue her lover.

Ereshkigal's Blessings

We ask your blessings
Ereshkigal

When we hear raised voices
remind us of the silence
of the earth.

When we see people without food
remind us of your oceans
of grain.

When we see death
remind us we all can expect
welcome.

Thank you for your blessings
Ereshkigal

Eagle Woman

The wind ruffles my hair.
I know you are near.
How high are you flying?
I cannot hope to see you
with my merely human eyes,
but I know I am seen.

Watch over me
As you would your own chick
as you would your own daughter,
my soaring mother. Ho!

Eagle Woman came to me, to my surprise, in meditation. She is one of the many bird-headed Goddesses. Sometimes you only know what she tells you. When the wind ruffles my hair, I know She is near.

Sedna Invocation

Sedna
Angry
We dare to see your face
We dare to see your pain
We dare to see your wounds

Sedna
Hear our words of comfort
Forgive the father and the husband who wounded you
Weep no more
Feel no pain

Immortal Sedna
Mother
Source of life
Food provider
Caretaker of the deep
We come to you
Come to us
Amen

To the Inuit people, Sedna dwells in the deep of the Arctic Ocean. Hers is moving story of betrayal and then transformation with the people who ask Her forgiveness and send Her comfort through their shaman.

Sarasvati's Song

Sweet flowing words
Blessings on the ears
Popping open the mind
To the heart's wisdom
And the soul's love.

With ease words come
To me her precious daughter
And to the lucky ones
Who hear her sweet voice
And know her open heart.

Brahma's Creation

From Brahma's chaos
The ordered universe comes
At the sweet direction
Of Ma Sarasvati's song.
See the beauty of Her wisdom
And Her loving heart.

The flowers bloom red and white
And petals fall
And scents drift on the breeze.
Who could plan this sweetness?
Sarasvati

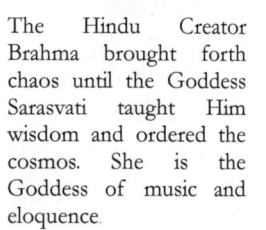

> The Hindu Creator Brahma brought forth chaos until the Goddess Sarasvati taught Him wisdom and ordered the cosmos. She is the Goddess of music and eloquence.

Aztec Mother Tonacacihuatl

Mother, Creator, Wife, Partner
You dared to join your power with the Divine Masculine,
Your husband Tonacatecuhtli
to bring forth this abundant Planet and all its creatures.
And when the earth was complete you created the skies
and all the magnificent bodies of light that fill it.
We marvel at what dreams you dreamt!
We are awestruck by the diverse, rich world you created.
What joy this creation must have been for you,
Mother of All!

But was there sadness too?
When you see the blueness of the sky, do you mourn the
green sky, the pink sky, the yellow sky that will never be?
When you see the carbon-based life forms,
do you mourn the crystal-based life forms
or the disembodied life-forms that will not be on this planet?

When a baby is born into this world,
do you mourn its death whether too soon or too late?
We mourn with you tonight.
We too mourn choices made that limited possibilities.
We too mourn dreams put aside unrealized.
We too mourn a loved child lost to death.
We mourn with you,
Mother Tonacacihuatl,
and ask you to care for the lost
children and dreams.

Despite the bloody image we have of the Aztecs, it takes only a little research to find this loving creator mother. In Mexico, people still beseech Her to comfort a child who has died.

Whirlpool Prayer

The whirlpool spins; a frightening and power force dragging us down into the depths. Ships are lost and hopes die in the vortex of water and darkness.

In these days of chaos and fear, with powerful forces pulling our planet and governments into hopeless collision and environmental destruction, we turn to you dear Goddess, Gyhldeptis, Lady Hanging Hair.

Call the spirits and powers, call the warriors and lovers, call the tribes of goodwill and nations of technology to the party.

We gladly join You dear Goddess in the feasting and the dance. Let it create the energy to channel the deadly whirlpool into the smooth flowing, life enhancing river.

Ho!

> Gyhldeptis, Lady Hanging Hair, is the goddess of the deep forest of two Pacific Northwest tribes. When a whirlpool threatens ships and costs many lives, Gyhldeptis hosts a feast and enlists the spirits to help. They change the whirlpool into a river.

Prayer to the Goddess of Tornadoes

If this be the day that I die,

I am at peace, for my Divine Mother Oya is waiting for me.

If this be the day that I die,

I willingly release my last breath into Her airy Being.

If this be the day that I die,

I soothe my panicked animal body with the knowledge that I will be home and safe soon.

If this be the day that I die,

I rejoice and I join Oya's powerful dance

as the winds of the heavens reach down and sweep me into the sky.

Oya is the Yoruban and Caribbean Orishi of air, wind, tornadoes, and hurricanes. Your first breath brings Oya into your life; your last breath lets your life go back to her.

Prayers of the Dark Days

It is wonderful to feel the free flowing connection to the Goddess and to explore that connection in joyous dialogue, but while living on this planet not all days are like that. We all face dark days when loneliness, sadness, anger, or other dark emotions block us from seeing Her presence. Here are some prayers from those dark days.

I Pray to the Loving God

I pray to the Loving God
Call her the Great Mother
Call her the Ancient Mother
For She is great and ancient
But mostly She is Mother.

All my loneliness
I give to Her
I don't know
What use She might have of it

I feel so large when
Her energy is passing through me
I feel so small, deflated, hollow after

Can I believe that She is with me then?

Is there a world where I am Her child every day?

The Mammogram Prayer

It never before mattered.
I never before worried.
It defined 'just routine.'

Routine changed
and my life
An odd bright shadow
A year of medicine

An anniversary
An appointment
A shadow of worry

Can I bear the news?

Oh God, let it be routine.

I am in Pain

Kwan Yin,
I feel pain in my body now.
I fear it growing.
I fear it lasting.
I fear its meaning.
I fear dying.

Kwan Yin,
I give this pain to you.
Please, stand between me and fear.
Ride this dragon for me.

Kwan Yin,
Thank you for hearing my prayer.
Thank you for handling my pain.

Kwan Yin,
I turn away from awareness of pain.
I turn away from all fearful thoughts.
I trust you to handle this
as I busy myself with things
I can do now.

Kwan Yin is the Chinese Goddess of Compassion. She is often shown standing on the back of a dragon demonstrating Her power over the dragon energy.

Being, Allowing

A friend saw me
holding out my hand
allowing the Goddess
to step onto the earth

My body was exhausted.
My mind fogged with chemicals.
I had only the strength
to be willing to surrender.
It was all the Goddess needed.

Let me learn the lesson
Be, allow,
The Goddess is here.

Holy Demon

Demon child
puny babe
hungry, so hungry
so lost, so vulnerable
unloved
alone

Where is your mother
Demon child?
Why can't she love you
Demon child?

Overflowing
aching breast
swollen nipple
painful fullness
seeking a mouth

Where is your mother
Demon child?
What doesn't she feed you
Demon child?

Nipple in mouth
need, pull too strong
greed, demand
flow too slow
too late
Where is your mother
Demon child?
Why doesn't her milk satisfy
Demon child?

Let go
let change
Pachamama
big as a mountain
big as the planet
milk abundant

Bridget
willing foster mother
fresh arms
sweet voice

Holy child
fed
satiated
sleepy
cuddled
quiet
loved

Holy Demon

Pachamama is the Peruvian Earth Mother.

Bridget is the Irish saint who miraculously acted as foster mother for the Christ Jesus on the night he was born in Bethlehem.

Tonacacihuatl

In Memory of Louis Ressijac

I remember my friend,

He has passed on to you.

Tonacacihuatl.

Lucky you to have him!

I miss him so

His wit

His vision

His care

We could talk for hours

And never be bored.

We could be silent together

And never be at a loss for words.

Why did he have to go?

So young

So needed

So kind

I miss him so

All these years

All these long years

Take good care of him,
Tonacacihuatl,
Surround him with people
Who love him
Who match his wits
Who respect his great heart.

Please, Tonacacihuatl,
Let his father embrace him
And understand all he is.
Let the barriers between them
Finally fall.

Let him watch me be a fine old crone.
It's what he wished for me in his last days
As he was dying young.

Take loving care of him,
Tonacacihuatl,
Until I can join him.

I miss him so.

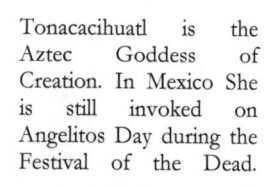

Tonacacihuatl is the Aztec Goddess of Creation. In Mexico She is still invoked on Angelitos Day during the Festival of the Dead.

Grandmother Bone Woman

I feel like crying
but the tears don't come.
No hurt or loss
is in my life.
What past hurt
needs tears—
I just don't know

The Dark Days

Your sweet, lined face
seems to understand
being haunted by sadness,
a life of losses
too big to mourn.

Grandmother
Bone Woman
put flesh on the bones
of my lost past.
Resurrect the loves
and joys
and dreams
that were too painful
to mourn.

As I sit
with your soft gaze upon me,
may I have the strength
to see the living presences
I thought were gone.
Let my eyes cry
my heart hurt
my nose run.
Let me sob or shout
or sing or move
until peace returns.

I know that peace
and freedom
and joy
will elude me
until the journey
is taken
and completed.

Help me, Grandmother.

More than one tradition tells of an old wise woman that can take the bones of the dead and bring them back to life. She is magic and appears mad, at times, but it is wisdom that allows Her to see reality as we can not see it-not madness.

The Dark Days

Evening News Prayer

Kali, Pele, Tara, Mary, Mothers and Powers all,
we your children call out to you in fear and self-loathing
as we look at the violence and destruction around us
as we hear of the wars and murders
as we watch the divine being used to justify slaughter.

Give us this day all your comfort and strength.

Transform our hearts and minds today
That our first thought is gratitude
That our first feeling is love
When we watch the evening news.

We thank you with all our hearts
for the marvelous world
You have created for our classroom
and playground.

Amen

Mary, Tara, and Kali are all Black Madonnas. They are portrayed with onyx black skin and represent timeless truth.

Mary is the virgin mother of the Christ Jesus. She is the Queen of Heaven and is known to answer all calls for help.

Tara is the mother of all Buddhas, healer and protector.

Kali is the Hindu Goddess that is the Destroyer of Illusion.

The Hawaiian Goddess of Volcanoes, Pele, is a powerful destructive force but she creates the land that allows life to come out of the ocean.

The Crowded Stairway

I own and claim the angry-me
Who curses, fumes, and fights.
I hold her hand as I climb
And love her all I can.

I own and claim the judging-me
Who grumbles, belittles, and blames.
I hold her hand as I climb
And love her all I can.

I own and claim the martyred-me
Who adds resentment to each act.
I hold her hand as I climb
And love her all I can.

I own and claim the fearful-me
Who cowers, cringes, and clings.
I hold her close as I climb
And love her all I can.

Murderers, muggers, terrorists, and despots,
No need to act it out!
I'll fight the war within my Self
And love me all I can.

God is good and God is great,
Her blessed child I am.
As I love me all I can
She loves me, all I am.

Prayer of the Wounded Child

Mommy, where are you?
I want you now!
I am hungry.
I am hurt.
I am cold.
I am tired.
I am scared.
I am confused.
I am lost.
Where is my mommy?
Why can't she hear me cry?
Will I be lost forever?
Mother, Mother, why hast thou forsaken me?

Mommy is here, Sweetie Pie,
Your life is my gift to you.
It is a gift with many flavors—
Not all are sweet.

Treat my precious child with tender love every day.
Yours are the hands I have to care for her.

Feed her well, she is hungry.
Comfort her, she is hurt.
Wrap her up, she is cold.
Put her to bed, she is tired.
Stand between her and harm, she is scared.
Calm the situation, she is confused.
Find her today, she is lost.

Mommy is here,
Sweetie Pie,
Find me every day.
Open yourself to my milk.
Feel yourself in my arms.

Everyday Prayers

Sometimes prayer is just a quiet personal communication from a woman just trying to get through her life. Prayer becomes a confiding or tantrum or plea or grumble or rant. Those may be the prayers of most power because they are the real bond between the human and the Divine. They are not elegant or public; they represent the true bond of the heart.

My days and worries and joys may be different than yours but, I hope, my humble prayers will show you how simple speaking to the Goddess may be.

Goddess Mother

It's a perfectly beautiful day!

Thank you for the sun, after the storm: the moderate temperature, after the heat.

This would be a perfect day to work in the garden, to enjoy the things growing and the rain softened soil.

So why do I feel grumpy and tired, depleted?

What dark corners
What doubts or dis-ease
Stands between me
and my enjoyment of the day?

I am willing to face the blocks.
I am willing to soften the walls.
I am willing to accept your light in all the dark places.

I ask you, Mother, for vibrant health and the support for the entire journey, or the instant of enlightenment, it will take to manifest it.

Amen

Ancient Mother

Source of Life

Spark of the World

Bless my family, friends, and neighbors today. May they all find moments of peace. May they experience joy. May they be blessed.

I am grateful for the amazing abundance of my life. After so many years of striving, I never thought I would have a time I didn't need to work hard for my daily bread.

I wish I felt totally—and only—the gratitude. But some part of me is still striving, still pushing for the breakthrough that would make me "enlightened" and always aware of your Divine Presence in my life.

I beat up on myself because my self-care is way less than perfect and the resultant body shows it. And I am ashamed, Mother, that this is the best I can do.

Bless me, Mother, for I have sinned. For penance I will work in my garden which is no penance at all.

I am your Beloved Child—I hope.

Mata Kali

Holy Moly, Mata Kali

Okay, I have this minor but irritating health problem. I have had it off and on for two years. I know all the symptoms, all the preventatives, all the ways to minimize the symptoms, all the curatives.

I was so pleased that the problem was completely cleared up for a whole week--maybe, even ten days. I thought (at last!) I had cleared the mind-set of the energy pattern. I was ready to move on to something else.

SO WHY IS THE SYMPTOM BACK TODAY?

Is this a punishment? Am I in the remedial spiritual growth class?

Okay, I know the drill—Thank you, Kali Ma, that this symptom is so minor and that I have all the support I need to deal with it. Thank you for facilitating my spiritual growth in such a gentle way. (Hey, in this Kali Yuga, you could have burnt down my house or put me in the hospital.) I affirm my intention to heal this symptom. I am vibrantly healthy.

Kali, Destroyer of Illusion, I request your power in my life to learn to destroy this illusion of ill health. I ask your loving support of my growth.

And, please, help me get over the grumpy way I feel today.

Your tired child

Your struggling devotee

Kali is the Hindu Goddess who is the Destroyer of Illusion. She is a fierce killer of demons. Yet she brings her husband back to life by merely walking on him. Her name means "Time" and she sees beyond the time of our lives to eternity. She is beautiful and terrible. Kali Yuga is an epoch in the cycle of time in which some Hindu scholars believe we are currently. It is a time of chaos that prepares for the coming epoch of growth.

Mother Oya

I could use your energy of change in my life today. Put the massive power of your hurricane behind my intent to improve my health. Knock down the old patterns or fears that are holding me back. Flatten the history that is so old I see it as truth when it is actually false. Allow the surging waves of positive energy to wash over me and through me. I am vibrantly healthy.

I pray that you help me to see the struggles of my friends and neighbors as their perfect path. I let go of my need to "fix" and "help." I support them by holding them in the light and calling you to bless them with sweet air. I see them as perfect, whole, and complete.

Thank you for clearing the air with the recent storms. It has made my garden and trees look wonderful.

Joy to the world!

Oya is the Yoruban and Caribbean Orishi of air, wind, tornadoes, and hurricanes. A babe's first breath brings Oya into its life; one's last breath lets your life go back to Her.

Dearest Goddess

In this drought, thank you for the blessing of rain. Even those few moments will sustain stressed trees and plants and shrubs.

I ask, with great confidence that I will be heard and answered, for support and guidance in this time of great change. I am open to change. I am willing for the world around me to change although I am terrified at the prospects at this moment.

Bless me with peace. Bless me with a sound sleep and profound dreams.

So mote it be.

Goodnight, Sarasvati!

Now I lay me down to sleep. Sleep is the operative word here, Goddess. I do not need to be awake in the middle of the night with the words, words, words cluttering my mind. How am I supposed to be awake and writing your book in the morning with no sleep!

Goddess of Eloquence, give me a break. I spent hours today writing and I am grateful for the flowing words you sent me. Now I need to rest my mind and body and recuperate so I can do more tomorrow. I am willing and eager to open up to your words—your inspiration—but I request you let me sleep the night through.

Sarasvati, you taught Brahma the wisdom to put things in order out of the chaos. Remember night is a time for rest and let me sleep, I pray you. If I am needed this night to serve the Divine purpose by lending my consciousness and energy to some work in this or another space or dimension, I willingly offer myself to serve. Just don't expect me to get much writing done if I wake up tired and grumpy.

Your admirer.

The Hindu Creator Brahma brought forth chaos until the Goddess Sarasvati taught Him wisdom and ordered the cosmos. She is the Goddess of music and eloquence.

Great Expectations

Grandmother,

I have great expectations for today. All the signs are there, say the astrologers, for a new beginning and profound change. Over millennia the ancients tracked the days, the stars, the courses of the planets, and predicted a new time.

Sitting in this woman's body, in this human life, in this moment, I don't see it. What change of mind or vision do I need to see this new day? I seem to be immersed in old psychological patterns. I still get the same old buttons pushed and the same old emotions push me toward the same old reactions.

Give me brownie points for seeing it as it happens! And I do stop before the reactions, sometimes. And I recognize the buttons. But I haven't been able to reset the buttons to play a new tune on the jukebox of my emotions. Yes, this is progress. It just doesn't feel like much progress!

Help me today, Wise Old Grandmother, to let go of expectations. Help me, instead, to be kind and gentle to myself. Heal the wounds that created the buttons and tunes of my life. Steer me to the places and people who will teach me new tunes.

All my gratitude to you, Grandmother, for giving me another day of life to find them.

Ancient Mother

The pure light of October shines on the brightly colored leaves—all the rich greens and golds. I love this time of year. I feel healthier in the mild days and cool nights.

I am reminded of friends lost as the leaves fall. I am reminded of dreams left behind and paths not taken. I ask you to help me lay them to rest today. Let them fall among the golden leaves and decay so that the soil is ready for seeds and inspiration.

I ask you, Ancient Mother, to inspire me. Give me words and rituals that will help me and my friends find peace and joy and abundance. If words and rituals are not what I need today, then I humbly ask you to give me what I really need to experience peace and joy and abundance. If what I need to grow today is not peace or joy or abundance, then I ask you, Loving Mother, to send the emotions and experience that will most benefit me and the planet today.

My peaceful place of prayer has just been invaded by a busload of grade school children on a field trip. Is that the answer to my prayer—screams and laughter, questions and demands? Who needs peace when there is enthusiasm and learning in the air? Not me, I guess.

Thank you for this answer.

Prayers for Special Occasions

As an interfaith minister I am sometimes called upon to lead prayers for people outside my Goddess Circle. Sometimes prayers are written for special services or special times of the year. Here are a few examples of how I respect these special occasions and opportunities.

Pour the Dew of Heaven—a Prayer on 9/11

Lady Kwan Yin
We know of your compassion
On this day of awful memory
We ask you to take away our fear.

Pour the dew of heaven
Into the hearts who are full of grief
Pour the dew of heaven
Into the hearts who are still fearful

Lady Kwan Yin
Compassionate One
We ask you to do what we cannot do
Pour the dew of heaven
Into the hearts who cheered at this horror

Lady Kwan Yin
May we all be done with division and violence.
May we all feel the love and peace of Nirvana.

Please.

Kwan Yin is a Buddhist Bodhisattva from China. A Bodhisattva is a human who has reached enlightenment and could move on to Nirvana but She vowed to not leave until all of us have gone before her. Her name means 'She who hears the cries of the world.' She is the Goddess of Compassion and the Goddess Who Takes Away Fear. Statues and paintings often show Her holding a vessel which contains the dew of heaven.

All Souls Day

Ancient Mother, Source of all Creation,
comfort us
as we remember our beloveds
who have passed over.

Help us to open to our beloveds
that we may continue to feel their love
and their presence in our lives.

Help us to heal the feelings
of loss and grief we felt at their passing,
feelings that linger with us
in our human lives.
Let us remember the joy of love
and experience it again
with loves lost and loves found again.

We look to you, Ancient Mother,
for comfort and love
beyond all others
but in this human life
we are grateful with all our hearts
for comfort and love of human arms
and we miss them when they pass on to you.

Mother, bless us, your weeping children.

Amen

Special Occasions

The Winter Solstice

On this longest night
we dare to look
at the darkness
for your loving face
Mary, Tara, Kali

Yes, you have a face
of light and color
seen in art and figure
full of sweetness
Mary, Tara, Kali

On this night we seek
the other face
the pure black face
of the cave, the womb
of the tormented night
Mary, Tara, Kali

Across eons and continents
they called you, Mother
seeing in your black face
the mystery, the answer, the love
needed on the longest night
Mary, Tara, Kali

We call you, Mother
Black Madonna
in the timeless darkness
of the longest night
seeking not comfort
but wisdom, understanding
beyond what our eyes can see
beyond the light
in your divine darkness
Mary, Tara, Kali

Mary, Tara, and Kali are all Black Madonnas. They are portrayed with onyx black skin and represent the timeless truth.

Mary is the virgin mother of the Christ Jesus.

Tara is the mother of all Buddhas.

Kali is the Hindu Goddess that is the Destroyer of Illusion.

Welcome Today

Welcome today
To all people of love and light.
To all people of openness and forgiveness.
To all people of hope.

Welcome today
To all sick people who pray for health.
To all poor people who pray for prosperity.
To all tired people who pray for rest.
To all imperfect people who are trying.

The Goddess welcomes each of you
With all Her heart
And, at this moment,
And, for all times,
She blesses you
With love
With light
With openness
With forgiveness
With hope
With health
With prosperity
With rest
With perfection

And She says,
"Welcome home."

Christmas Eve Invocation

This is the night before.

This is the time when the growth within has been completed but is not yet manifest.

The Mother, and the Father, await the birth in joy and terror at this new beginning for the child and for them.

In memory of that night so long ago when they awaited the coming of the child, we invite Mother Mary and Father Joseph to join us this evening.

We honor you Mary: young woman, new wife, mother of a child within, holy being touched by God.

We honor you Joseph: mature man, carpenter, new husband, bemused man who has been touched by miracle.

Mary and Joseph, help us to understand the place of human beings in the life of God as we celebrate this last moment before the Child of Light becomes manifest.

Amen

Back to School Prayer

Ancient Mother, we your children greet you with joy and gratitude. We thank you, with full hearts, for all the blessings that you have granted us this week.

Ancient Mother, at this time of year, time of new beginnings, for children and their anxious parents, we ask you to watch over each child on its way to school. May this time in each child's life be full of the joy of discovery and the confidence that new things can be learned and new skills developed with cheerful, diligent practice.

Ancient Mother, we ask you to bless each adult with the same joy and anticipation of learning. Let us all be thankful for this wondrous, complex world and the fabulous possibilities of our spiritual paths. May we skip along our paths to you like a kindergartener on her first day of school.

Amen.

After the Storm

I thank you, Oya,
that I am safe
my home is sound
my friends okay
the world fresh
and lovely
after the storm.

I thank you, Kali,
that I am recovered
my soul group safe
my joys possible
after the trauma.

I thank you, Pele',
that I am on solid ground
new possibilities open
the view different
mind expanded
after the upheaval.

I thank you, Mary,
that I am here
new light shines
peace floods the senses
after the birth.
Thank you.

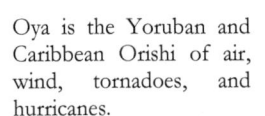

Oya is the Yoruban and Caribbean Orishi of air, wind, tornadoes, and hurricanes.

Kali is the Hindu Goddess that is the Destroyer of Illusion.

The Hawaiian Goddess of Volcanoes, Pele', is a powerful destructive force but She creates the land that allows life to come out of the ocean.

Mary is the virgin mother who gave birth to the Light that is the Christ Jesus.

Consecration

In the presence of the One God
Grandmother, Grandfather, Great Spirit
God the Father, the Son, and Holy Spirit
The Goddess, Maiden, Mother, and Crone

In the presence of the prophets and teachers
Jesus the Christ
Mohammad (May he be blessed)
The Buddha

In the presence of the unseens
the ancestors, angels, guides, spirits
In the presence of these people gathered
old friends and new, family, leaders, healers,
musicians, teachers, ministers

We consecrate this land and building.
May all who come here be welcome.
May all who come here be home.
May all who come here find what they seek.

If any come in sorrow, may they find comfort.
If any come in fear, may they find safety.
If any come lonely, may they find companionship.
If any come hurt, may they heal.
We thank the One God for answering this prayer.

We ask that this congregation be blessed
in all its actions for the good of all.
May any misunderstanding lead to new understanding.
May any strife lead to creativity.
May any anger fuel positive change.
May our prayers for health and prosperity be answered
beyond our wildest imaginings.

We thank the One God for this land and this chapel.
We thank the One God with all our hearts for each other.
Amen

The Gardener's Prayer

turn the soil.
add the manure.
plant the seed.
mulch.
water.
weed.
pick the flower.
put it in a vase.
put it on Her altar.

This is my prayer.

Begin your own Dialogue with the Goddess

Sharing someone else's prayers can be very moving and help open the pathways to the Divine, but no one's prayers are as powerful as your own. Prayer is our personal dialogue with the Divine. Our culture, unfortunately, seems to create a lot of barriers to the open dialogue with the Divine. Here are some of the barriers that I encountered and suggestions to dissolve them.

The True, Correct Name

When I began to study the Goddess, I became very frustrated that I couldn't find a specific Goddess's correct name and story. Not only would the Goddesses have different names, there were contradictory tales of Her. Somehow I believed one of them must be the right one and others wrong.

One day I was reading a book on the Hindu Goddess Kali. In the book were three pages of names for Her. The book described which name was used when you wanted to invoke a specific aspect or energy of Kali Ma. Suddenly, I realized that all the names were true and correct. All the many names just help our small human consciousness to perceive, for a moment, one aspect of the unfathomable expanse that is the Divine Feminine.

My joy of studying the Goddess expanded as I stopped looking for the correct name or story and began to look for Truth in every name, in every tale.

The Best Source

When I started studying the Goddess in the 1970's, it was hard to find information about the Goddesses. Many more books are available now and the World Wide Web makes it incredibly easy to find information. Yet not all the information to be found is meaningful or useful.

Some of the information is quite scholarly and dry. Some sources have little depth and make a goddess sound like a cartoon character. You can also find sources that describe a goddess and practices of Her devotees for the sole purpose of belittling or contesting their beliefs. Some tales of a specific goddess are retold by someone outside of her culture of origin and just don't seem very plausible when you think about it. None of these were necessarily helpful for someone on a spiritual path. Keep looking.

I found that I could soon learn to absorb enough about a specific goddess that I could discern the form and structure of her tale. I look for the Truth that is the basis for the story. This is done through a process of reflection and meditation that allows the name, tale, and energy of a specific goddess to be present in my life until I hear or see the Truth that she is bringing to me at that time.

Meditation on a Goddess can take a lot of forms. I am not one for sitting and quieting my mind—that only seems to make my mind spin more out of control. I keep pictures and statues of Her around me so She is called to mind often. Often a ritual or theme about the Goddess comes to me as I awake in the morning or drive somewhere or garden or do Qi Gong. As you begin opening to the Goddess, you will develop your own way to recognize Her message.

If I study the same goddess at two different times, I can become aware of very different facets of Her. This is the true richness of a dialogue with the Goddess.

A Goddess in Context

The name and tales of a Goddess comes from a people with language, culture, and history that may be very different than our own. To understand their Goddesses it can be very helpful to learn something of the people and how they lived. This can be quite an interesting journey into the spiritual paths of other peoples.

Serqet is the Egyptian Goddess of the Water Scorpion. How can we appreciate Her unless we know the impact of water scorpions in the daily lives of ancient Egyptians?

Not all Goddesses are Goddesses

Many religions and cultures, living and ancient, explore the Divine through worship of Goddesses. Others have ways of exploring that which is beyond themselves using different words and ways of looking at the spiritual or energy pattern beyond our own.

One of the most popular "Goddesses" in the US is the Chinese Buddhist Goddess Kwan Yin. She isn't a goddess at all. To the Buddhists, she is a woman who has achieved the knowledge and spiritual power of enlightenment while still alive. She decided not to enter Nirvana but to stay in this world. She vowed to help all others until they also achieve enlightenment. In the Buddhist tradition she is called a Bodhisattva. To the Buddhist, a Bodhisattva is more likely to be called upon than a deity who is seen as capricious and untrustworthy.

The Native Americans don't believe in Goddesses as we use the term but they tell stories of wise ancestor women that have unique powers and teach the people useful skills like weaving and rituals like the sweat lodge. They talk of the Great Spirit and call out to Grandmother and Grandfather when they address the Divine. This grounded approach can teach those of us on a spiritual path a different way to experience the Divine Feminine.

For the Yoruba of Africa, God is one and unknowable. In order for humans to appreciate God, they have described 401 manifestations of Divine energy which they call Orishi. These are named and described as humans but they represent an energy that is around us and accessible to us. Two hundred are destructive energies; two hundred are creative or preserving energies; and one is neutral. One I love is the Orishi Oya who is the moving air of breath--and tornadoes and hurricanes. She is the Goddess of sudden change.

Begin your own Dialogue

Letting go of the forms of the religions and cultures and looking for the common yearnings of the Divine Feminine can be very rewarding. In this book I refer to all of versions of the Divine Feminine as Goddesses and am very grateful for the expansion of my understanding of the Divine Feminine these other paths have given me.

Darshan

Darshan is the Sanskrit word for sight. It is a term used for a spiritual practice of looking into the eyes of the Divine. I think of it as "I see the Goddess; the Goddess sees me."

In learning about the Goddess, I found wonderful paintings and statues created of Her going back to the beginning of recorded time and beyond and around the world. One way to learn of the Goddess is to meditate on the images devotees have created of Her. For example, Ahset (who is more commonly known by Her Greek name Isis) is powerful and mysterious but I learned a sweeter quality of Ahset when I saw a tomb painting that showed Ahset leading the deceased woman gently by the hand.

Hundreds of paintings of the Buddhist Goddess White Tara show her seated in exactly same position. What does the raised left hand holding a lotus blossom between Her left thumb and ring finger mean to all those artists? If you explore this you can learn so much about how Her devotees perceive Her.

The art picturing the Goddess can be technically wonderful or it can be crude and awkward. But even the crude images tell us of the belief and devotion of the artists and what the Divine meant to them. Let them all be a channel for the Goddess to speak to you.

Some traditions require that the devotee make the image of the Divine with their own hands. Think how precious to an earthly mother are the things made for her by her children. Making an image no matter how fine or crude can be a lovely prayer to the Goddess.

Letting a Goddess Pick You

For years I have been creating a Goddess ritual circle each month honoring a different Goddess each time. For a long time I thought I was picking the Goddess. Then, I began to realize the Goddess was picking me. Her presence was perfect for the next step in my spiritual growth or to support me in my path. For instance, I was putting the final touches on the ritual for Hindu Goddess Lakshmi and wanted another story about Her when I found the story of Her cutting off Her breast so She could lay it on the altar of Lord Krishna. Since I found this story the day after I was diagnosed with breast cancer, it seemed an amazing gift to be shown a way to make my life a gift to the Divine.

Women often ask me what Goddess to turn to and then talk to me at great length about a Goddess whose statue that they just happen to have or who has been in their lives in many ways for a long time. If that is true for you, start with Her. If a Goddess is making Herself known to you, accept the invitation.

The Living Goddess

I was raised within a religion that had a long history and much learning and dogma. I found this upbringing unconsciously guided my approach to the Goddess. I was looking for the truth in books and rituals that others had created. It took decades of stumbling around before I realized I had a perfect source of information about a Goddess—Her.

It is not easy to open to this direct approach when we have been taught that all of the prophets who saw god are dead and we are to read their, often rather bizarre, stories and learn about god from old books. What?

I stumbled upon my path by creating a Goddess Circle once a month. I studied a Goddess and then tried to think up ways to adapt Her rituals or prayers to my circle of women. As time went on I became more accustomed to getting images of rituals—from out of the blue! I began to recognize the Goddess as the source from whom these images came.

Then, I began ask the Source and expect the Source to come up with the bright idea when I needed it.

You have to find your own way but do not be afraid to start the journey. From one who has gone down the path, I assure you that the journey is possible and worth the effort.

If you desire to know the Goddess, it does not matter what name you call Her. It does not matter what tradition or religion leads you to Her. Open yourself to her in prayer and meditation. Watch for Her presence in your life.

May I suggest a prayer?

"Mother, Source of all Creation, I am listening."

Hearing the Goddess

In order to have a dialogue communication must flow both ways. To pray with no expectation of receiving an answer may be traditional but is not what I have been seeking. This section may be why I had to wait until my 60s to write this book. Learning to hear the Goddess is a challenge in our noisy world where we are taught that all the prophets are long dead with their words captured in old books translated into formal, static language.

The first challenge is to believe it is possible to hear the Goddess and start listening. That simple idea embodies its own confusion. Listening and hearing imply words or music which may or may not be the way the Goddess communicates to us. It may be more accurate to say 'opening yourself to perceiving the Goddess' or 'allowing yourself to become aware of Her in your life'. These may be more accurate but are a whole lot more vague. This first challenge then becomes to believe that if you open the dialogue with the Goddess She will be communicating to you in answer. Let me affirm: the Goddess hears and answers.

The second challenge is listening. Listening takes practice. Babies are not aware that their mothers are saying things to them or they are so busy fussing that they do not stop and suck on the nipple in their mouths. We are like babies who are unaware that their mothers are speaking to them, so busy fussing that they do not realize that the comfort of the nipple they seek is already in their mouths. We are babies who need to relax and root around for the blessing, the answer, that has been sent. It is there somewhere.

Words

There are many forms the answers to our prayers can take. The most simple may be words in our minds. After a month of trying to pronounce the name of the Goddess Tonacacihuatl, I casually thought, "Can I have a Goddess whose name I can pronounce for next month's Goddess?" And I heard clearly in my mind, "Can you pronounce Cynthia?" Since I knew

Cynthia was a Roman Goddess and certainly can pronounce Her (and my) name, I knew I was answered. It was easy for me to realize this rather wry question was a message because I have been practicing this for decades. I remember very clearly the first time I got one of these communications. One October afternoon when I was in my 30's, I had gone to get a massage and the therapist mentioned that she was letting spirit give her a workshop that week. She had cleared her morning schedule and each morning asked spirit what she should do and did it. On the drive home, I wondered, "What would spirit say, if I asked what I should do?" And I heard, "Throw a birthday party for yourself!" I was very startled as this was October and my birthday is in January. Being startled helped me to sense the outside source for this idea. I decided to throw the party and it ended up being the most remarkable time for me and a turning point for my life. This reinforced that I could get wonderful results if I asked and allowed myself to hear and act on the answers.

I learned the pattern when words come from the Goddess. I ask casually. If I am worried or desperate, that gets in the way of hearing. When something offbeat, wry, funny, out-of-the-blue, uncharacteristic of me, is heard in my mind, I consider it—twice. What is needed to make it happen comes easily to me and the results are unexpectedly good. Let's go back to my birthday party. The idea to throw a party was not something in my mind as my birthday was months away. I had long ago given up on throwing parties for my birthday since it is a common day for a snow storm. I could think of a lot of reasons why it might be scary or painful to throw the party: *What if no one came! It would be work. I don't have a big enough place.* I could go on. This time, I decided to heed the voice. I talked to my massage therapist about the party since she had a house that was great for entertaining. She and her house mates agreed to throw the party for a fee to which we easily agreed. The results impacted my whole life. That is the pattern of the answered prayer: a casual question, an out-of-the-blue answer, internal backtalk, easy accomplishment, and then a profound result all out of proportion to the question or my actions.

Serendipity

Words are not the only way that the Goddess communicates. Another way is coincidence or serendipity. Years ago I went to a financial planner. After we worked together to create my financial plan to include long range plans for retirement and short range plans for vacations to exotic places, she gave me the information for five mutual funds in which to invest. I said to her, "If I have money for five mutual funds then I have enough to go on a cool vacation." She laughed at me and said, "Sure." That night in the mail I found a brochure about a trip to Peru. I decided that was where I wanted to go, but when I started trying to make it happen, I found I could not get a passport in time and could not get that particular time off work. I was very disappointed but I decided to go ahead and get the passport. Shortly after my passport arrived, I received another brochure about a different trip to Peru with a spiritually oriented group. Because I had my passport, I was able to go and had the most amazing experience. That pattern of something falling into your hands at a specific time to move you forward is also characteristic of a prayer being answered.

Once I asked the Goddess to let more exercise into my life. The next week I got a notice in the mail of a Qi Gong class being taught a block from my house. No excuses left. I loved the class and am still able to include Qi Gong in my life. The trick in this example was that I had to be aware that the message from the Goddess was on the way so I paid attention to the notice in the mail! "Listening" is a particular kind of paying attention to what comes into your life.

Another time I decided I was ready to find a community that would support my spiritual life and asked for help from the Goddess to find one that would fit my admittedly unusual perspective on the Divine. I decided to start looking. I picked up a new age magazine and found a little chapel in the same building as the Qi Gong class. I decided it would be as good place as any to start looking. I went to a Sunday morning service wearing a goddess necklace. The Pastor saw it and told me they had a Goddess Circle in which I might be interested. It was not quite that easy for this introvert to become part of that chapel, but I found this community was open to me and supported my path in ways I never expected. My participation in that chapel led me to my ministry and to writing this book.

There are many examples of happy accidents the Goddess has put in my path. A book falls off my bookcase as I brush by just happens to be the perfect reading for my next sermon. I decide to clean out a box of paper and find a meditation I had been saving for 25 years that would be great at the next Sunday Service I was leading. A meditation leader at my yoga studio reads a poem that would be perfect for my next Goddess Circle. Once you get accustomed to "listening," it is amazing how often what you need comes to you with ease.

Visions

Visions are a way the Goddess communicates to Her devotees. Since I am more a visual person than a word person, it did not surprise me that I would "see" the answers to my prayers. Visual images will arise when I am planning a Goddess ritual. With my mind's eye, I will see the group performing some action, walking outside, washing our hands, dancing, standing in a Goddess pose, lighting candles, singing, sitting in the dark. These visions come for me often when I am driving or weeding or otherwise doing something that busies my mind without challenging it. I am not very good at clearing my mind in meditation. I found that focusing on my body in yoga and Qi Gong or doing quiet household tasks or walking in beauty help me to soften my mind to receive the visions.

Visions can also come when preparing to sleep or awakening in the morning, if your mind is not crowded with the day's issues. I often awake with a poem or prayer in my mind and need only to write it down. The Mammogram Prayer was written that way.

Praying before you sleep is a classical way to prime the dialogue with the Goddess. You can even ask Her to give you ideas in dreams—but that is another whole book.

People

People can be answers to prayers. There is a Buddhist saying, "When the student is ready, the teacher will appear." It may be reasoned that everyone that appears in your life is the teacher for which you are ready. Of course, some of these 'teachers' are a there to teach very difficult lessons. The lessons are not difficult because they must be painful but because the easy ways were tried and we missed the lesson. Pain may be the only way to focus our attention on a lesson we have been avoiding.

I find it hard to give you the examples of this working in my life, not because I do not have examples in mind but because the people who have been my most powerful 'teachers' do not need to been seen in light of my life but in the light of their own. Let me give you two little examples.

One spring I planted a crabapple tree next to the street in my front yard. I love trees and nothing gives me more pleasure than planting one and seeing it grow. But after a trying day at work one afternoon, I was out watering my tree in the oppressive August heat and feeling very grumpy. A man drove by in a beat up old truck. He slowed for a speed bump and stuck his beefy arm and hairy head out of the window and yelled, "Grow, little tree, grow." It was so unexpected. I was so moved. In an instant, I let go of the bad day and the oppressive heat. Yes, that was why I was out there: grow, little tree, grow. I remember that so often with joy even though my little tree is now 20 feet tall!

When I was in chemo for breast cancer, I reached a place in my journey through Cancerland when I was so anemic I had to go back to bed and rest after getting up and dressing and eating breakfast. For a person like me that was always busy doing and creating and planning and running things this was awful. I thought of these days as slug days—days when I was useless. During these dark days, my friend Reverend Jane Batt told me of a vision she had of me. The Goddess was standing on a crescent moon that came down near the earth. I was standing on the ground and reached up to Her and took Her hand and She stepped onto the earth. Jane's vision and her reporting it to me allowed me to see what I could not see in my life before, certainly not when I was well and busy nor when lost in chemo fog, that I served the Goddess simply by being on the earth and reaching for Her. Flat on my back and unable to think or do, barely able to see to my own daily needs, I was serving the Goddess.

Since I could not "listen" at this time myself, the Goddess sent a messenger.

People can serve you and teach you in so many ways. They reflect who you are and what you allow. If you are doing everything alone, it is because you do not allow people to help. Now that was a hard lesson for me to learn. This book is living proof that I learned the lesson. When I was willing to let people help, there they were, willing and able and already present in my life. That too is how you "hear" the Goddess.

Knowing

Sometimes when the Goddess communicates to us, we just know. I am not sure how to describe this inner knowing that is not of the mind. I am not one to allow these knowings to go unexamined or unquestioned. To me earthly life has to be grounded in earthly thought as well as the spiritual. One of my teachers, healer Dennis Adams used say, "don't let spirit balance your checkbook." I examine my knowing on many levels but sometimes I just know.

One month I was preparing a Goddess Circle honoring the Hindu Goddess Kali. I saw many wonderful statues and paintings of Her on the World Wide Web. I wanted to buy one and had plenty of time to do so but I *knew* that I had to make Her image with my own hands. This was my last month before I was to retire. I had out of town company coming to celebrate. I did not want one more thing on my to-do list, but I accepted this *knowing* and made an image of Kali for the service. It turned out to be quite a project taking artist-skills and creativity, as well as engineering to support the heavy weight of the image within the frame. The image I created worked fine for the service as any image might have done. What creating this image did for me was to help me understand that I was not leaving my engineering self behind as I left my career, but taking it with me as I embarked on a new phase of my life. This was a lovely reassurance at a time I needed it.

Accepting the Message

All my life I have been waiting for the message from god to shave my head and go live in a cave. It amuses me how often the message I actually receive from the Goddess has been one of comfort and ease. She does not ask me to sacrifice but to luxuriate. Since this was not the message I was expecting, it took me a very long time to hear it.

The reassuring part of my dialogue with the Goddess is that She does not give up. She will keep communicating. We get the answer to our prayers, every day. And some days we even hear them. Some days, we even recognize them.

On the Goddess Path

I love the Goddess. It was very long journey on the path from the frightening god of my childhood to a wonderful presence that is now in my life. I stumbled through many rough patches moving slowly in Her direction. I was looking for a god in whose image I was made. I tried New Age groups. They moved me forward with self-development and learning about the power of thought and affirmations but did not satisfy my mystic self that longed for the Divine. I tried the Wicca and loved the Goddess focus and the ties to nature and natural cycles but found the rituals didn't relate to my life and supported duality in a way that made me very uncomfortable. The first time a group leader tried to lead us in a curse I balked. Cursing even rapists did not seem like a path to the spiritual life I sought. I studied the Motherpeace and Daughters of the Moon Tarot Decks and was thrilled to see the Divine Feminine in so many varied and powerful forms from cultures around the world reaching back far into the history of humankind. It whetted my appetite for more. I wanted to know about Her but I also wanted to experience interaction with Her in ritual and prayer--mystical experiences!

Over seven years ago I began creating and leading a monthly circle to honor the Goddess at the Takoma Park Chapel in Silver Spring, Maryland. Each month I would pick a different Goddess. This commitment disciplined me to focusing on Her seriously and regularly. I would study Her and the culture and religion from which She came through the internet and books. Preparing a monthly service exercised my ability to open to intuition, inspiration, and creativity. I became more and more confident that I would at some point 'see' the perfect ritual or the perfect picture or the idea for a meditation or prayer would show up. Through my experiences and those of the wonderful people who joined me, I was encouraged to keep exploring and learning about the Goddess.

This is what I learned.

In Her Image

The Divine is not embodied. It is not male or female. Humans have always pulled the Divine into human form to help them imagine and relate to the amazing and powerful and awe-inspiring enormity that is the Divine. Each of the Goddesses I studied was there to wedge open my mind and heart to some aspect of the incomprehensible whole that is the Divine. Each story being told was a humble human-sized lesson for a immensity that could not fit in one story or book or life. Each Goddess and Her story can be savored for the small taste of the Divine in among the human trappings. This may not be easy as some of the stories are harsh in the extreme, but when you reach the moment of when the Divine shines through, it is worth all the thought and time.

Being born female in a culture and time that did not value the feminine, I wanted a female god. I wanted my femininity valued and honored. I did not want to be a virgin or whore or mother. I wanted to see the characteristics of woman being seen as a reflection of the Divine and not just an inspiration to sin. The young feminist me wanted to have some support from on high! And I found it, if not in any way I could have imaged. I found Goddesses who were warriors, sluts, witches, magicians, mothers, adulterers, destroyers, creators. I found Goddesses who were wives and others who lived solitary lives. I found Goddesses of those traditionally 'womanly arts' in the hearth and home and Goddesses who conquer on the battlefields and others who set the cosmos spinning. I could be made in the image of the Goddess—and I could be anything.

Humor

I have always taken the Divine rather seriously and thought the Divine took itself rather seriously. Then the ancient Japanese Goddess Uzume dropped in on my life. Only two stories are known about Her, and in both cases She handled the problems no one else could solve by baring her breasts and generally behaving outrageously. When I read of Her, I laughed. I realized some part of me had still believed that god would reward me for being a good little girl, and that meant modest and demure and quiet (although I have to admit I was never particularly good at being a good little girl). Here was a Goddess whose femaleness was not restrained, not harnessed by the cultural rules. I am sure that is why She was known as the Most Alarming Female in Heaven. Uzume used Her femaleness to help and protect others without restraint or taking Herself seriously. In the very ordered hierarchy of the Japanese depiction of the Divine, Uzume stands out like a disco ball splashing Her humorous light all over everyone.

Compassion

There are many wonderful loving Goddesses that express the scope of compassion that is Divine. The one that taught me the most about compassion is the Chinese Goddess Kwan Yin. Her stories include Her coming to the aid of people in peril, protecting children, and even letting her hands to be cut off to make a drink that would save her dying father. Her compassion is not limited to those big-eyed small creatures that open all of our hearts. Her heart is large enough to feel love for even the abusers of the world.

When I first read Kwan Yin's Prayer for the Abuser, I realized that Divine Compassion was far beyond my own humble limits of compassion for those around me. It was perfect and without prejudice. It was complete. It was compassion that knew exactly the person's heart and could accept every part of the person, good, bad, and totally depraved. And I knew that there was no part of me that this Goddess could or would not accept. I also began to understand that I did not have to earn Divine Compassion. I could be assured it would be there for me and for all those around me.

Power

A word of warning: Don't pray to the Goddess if you are not ready for change in your life. The Goddess is powerful. Her power can change everything. Yoruban Goddess Oya, for instance, can solve that little problem of overstuffed closets; She is after all the Goddess of Tornadoes and Sudden Change and can have those closets cleaned out in seconds—and the whole house with it. I write this in jest, in part, but I also understand the power of this image when I want a change in my life and feel weighted down with thoughts of how hard it will be. Say a little prayer to Oya and let Her power push you out of that rut and move you on your way.

The Hawaiian Goddess Pele' is a great example of the immense power that is both destruction and construction. She is the Goddess of Volcanoes and we know that when the volcano erupts there is little we mere humans can do to stop the path of destruction of the lava and ash clouds. But the other side of this coin is that the Hawaiian Islands would not have arisen out of the unimaginable depths of the Pacific Oceans and formed land upon which lush life exists without these volcanoes.

Oya and Pele' are myths that embody huge natural forces. The people that describe these Goddesses understand the power of the Divine to create, destroy, and change our world. However much science can explain the mechanics of tornadoes and volcanoes, it cannot explain the Divine.

Many Goddesses are fierce protectors, particularly of women and children. Mother Durga, the Hindu Goddess, defeats the armies of the demons who have been harming humans when all the Gods under Lord Shiva have been unable to do so. When She is done fighting, She leaves, even after being asked to stay and rule, but as She leaves She promises to return if called. The Mother of all Buddhas Tara protects people from thieves and snakes. The Egyptian Goddess Serqet protects against water scorpions. Each Goddess protects Her people from the threat in their daily lives.

Goddesses also have the power to comfort and heal. The Divine Mother is the unconditionally loving, care-taking mother each child deserves and doesn't have in its human mother. She never gets tired; Her attention never falters. She is as big as a mountain, as big as the planet. She provides everything we need without stinting. This loving Mother is the most common portrayal of Her. This is the unique power of the Divine Feminine.

Kwan Yin's Prayer for the Abuser

(Author Unknown)

To those who withhold refuge, I cradle you in safety at the core of my Being.

To those that cause a child to cry out, I grant you the freedom to express your own choked agony.

To those that inflict terror, I remind you that you shine with the purity of a thousand suns.

To those who would confine, suppress, or deny, I offer the limitless expanse of the sky.

To those who need to cut, slash, or burn, I remind you of the invincibility of Spring.

To those who cling and grasp, I promise more abundance than you could ever hold onto.

To those who vent their rage on small children, I return to you your deepest innocence.

To those who must frighten into submission, I hold you in the bosom of your original mother.

To those who cause agony to others, I give the gift of free flowing tears.

To those that deny another's right to be, I remind you that the angels sang in celebration of you on the day of your birth.

To those who see only division and separateness, I remind you that a part is born only by bisecting a whole.

For those who have forgotten the tender mercy of a mother's embrace, I send a gentle breeze to caress your brow.

To those who still feel somehow incomplete, I offer the perfect sanctity of this very moment.

Sensuality

Coming from the religion and culture that divorces spirituality from the physical, it was charming to find Goddesses that celebrate the sensual. The Yoruban Goddess Oshun is the Goddess of sweet flowing water. She is often shown wading in a stream. She is also the Goddess of self-adornment. She is shown in beautiful costume and jewelry looking at Herself in a hand mirror. There is something very sweet about this quality of primping and admiring oneself being seen the Divine. So when I am having a perfect hair day and it makes me smile in my mirror I am merely reflecting the beauty of the Goddess.

The Egyptian Goddess Bast is a woman with the head of a cat. All cats were sacred to her. She embodied the sensual qualities of cats: the stretching, the napping, the grace of movement, the cleanliness, the always knowing where to lay that makes her look the best. (Well, my cat Lady always knew.) This joy in embodiment is so refreshing to someone raised without it in my deity.

Sex

Let's not forget sex. In many stories of the Divine, the Goddesses are paired with a God that is husband

and/or brother to Her. Creation becomes an act of sexual ecstasy—or a game between them. The Hindus are famous for their erotic temple art that demonstrates this potential. They certainly aren't the only ones. The Chinese Creatrix Nu Kua set the cosmos in motion with her brother/husband Fu Hsi.

The most famous of the wife Goddesses may be the Egyptian Goddess Ahset (often known by her Greek name Isis) and her brother/husband Osiris. The painful story of how Ahset lost her beloved husband and searched for all the pieces of him and magically animated him for one last night so She could bear his child must wring the heart of so many women.

The ancient Mesopotamian Goddess Inanna and the Greek Goddess Aphrodite are Goddesses of love and sexuality but notably not Mother Goddesses. Certainly the beauty and sensuality and sexiness of Aphrodite have lived on into our own culture if not the understanding of Her Divinity.

Good Behavior

What is good behavior and why do the goddesses behave so badly? Pele' fell in love with someone else's husband and killed her rival. Her brother came and lectured Her until She saw that what She had done was wrong. She showed Her remorse by turning the husband into a tree and the wife into a lovely vine that always grows entwined around that tree. The Goddess Kali goes berserk on the battlefield and starts killing everything until She sees Her beloved husband among the dead. She then dances on his body and brings is back to life. Neither of these are models of 'good behavior' but they both demonstrate that some behavior is unacceptable and remorse leads to attempts at reparation.

Some stories seem to tell us what the Goddesses consider good behavior by what they reward and punish. The Celtic Goddess Bridget had two men with a terrible skin disease come to Her sacred spring. She told one to take the water of Her spring and put it on the skin of his companion. When he had cleaned his companion's skin with water from the spring, his companion was cured. When the Goddess directed the cured man to put Her water on his diseased companion's skin, he refused fearing that he would catch the disease again. The Goddess stepped in and gave him the disease again and cured the other man.

In the Native American traditions, women came and taught the people how to behave. For instance, White Buffalo Calf Woman taught practical skills but also gave the Lakota seven rituals including the peace pipe and vision quests and sweat lodges to help them live their lives in harmony. In the beginning, Spider Woman helped the Dinah and Hopi emerge from the ground and taught them survival skills and how to weave.

The Goddess has not given us commandments in stone. The Wiccan say, first, do no harm and do as you will. This is simpler to say than to do when you include doing no harm to all the creatures of the earth and the earth Herself.

In studying the Goddess in many traditions, I have found that She is not about rules but about love, for others and for yourself.

Meaning of Life and Death

The most astounding lesson that the Goddess experiences has given me is that the actions of one life, no matter how wonderful or how egregious, are not important to the Divine Mother. Her knowledge of us spans over time much, much longer than one life. Death is no ending.

The Hindu Goddess Kali, whose skin and hair are the gleaming onyx black of the infinite, dances in the crematorium grounds to welcome souls as they journey to the next phase. Her name means 'Time' to remind us that our lives are mere blinks to Her. How we live one life, who we appear to be, and how we behave is immaterial because we will be many people and behave in many ways over the eons. Death is merely the momentary shift to the new experience.

The Ancient Mother in many of Her forms does not reward or punish lives but encourages and supports the lessons we need to learn. Her attitude about us is of a mother who sends her children out to play.

Does she love the one who plays cop over the one who plays robber? The cowboy over the Indian? (or vice versus) Luke Skywalker over Darth Vader? She just watches the way we throw ourselves into our parts with astounding courage and drive and belief and she smiles, awaiting the time for us to come home for dinner and an encouraging word. And, yes, some of us will surely need a bath.

The comfort of the image of the all-loving Mother God doesn't satisfy our troubled minds when we see terrible things happen to people. When studying the amazing African Goddess Mawu, I found a story of a messenger She sent to spend a day on earth. The messenger killed a child, burnt a house, and drowned an old man so a young man could become king in his place. Each occurrence seemed awful and cruel. But at the end of the story the messenger explains how the good of all depended on these occurrences. I struggled with whether to include this harsh story but in the end I realized how important it is to understand that what we see and know from our human perspective is not what is seen by the Divine.

Another Goddess gives a sweet way to look at life and its end. The Goddess Oya, the Goddess of Air, moves into us with our first breath and our spirits join her with our last exhale. This lovely and comforting thought allows us to see how the Divine enlivens us each moment and is our source from which we come and to whom we return.

Finding Her Presence

Most of the above are things I learned in studying the many Goddesses. They have profoundly changed my thinking and feelings about the Divine and about me, but this is humble compared to the times I have felt Her Presence.

One day, that I will never forget, I was at Sunday Service at the Takoma Park Metaphysical Chapel. We were concentrating our energies on spiritual healing of those who felt dis-eased. I was standing at the back of the room holding the energies that were pouring into the group. I became aware of an amazing vibrating energy that seemed to fill my body and expanded as if I were a balloon being blown up until I was several times larger than my real, round body. Words filled my mind. Each word and sentence was avidly observed and selected from among the possibilities. Each new sentence added when the previous thought was seen as incomplete. I was filled with intense emotion as I reacted to the words sorting themselves in my mind. Suddenly they were done, ready. I wondered if there was someone I was going to meet that needed to hear these words. Then, I thought, "What, you want me to say them now?!" I struggled with this because I was merely attending this service and someone else was the focus. Even though the chapel was silent at the time, I clearly understood that now was the time.

My voice spoke the words but I didn't sound like me to my own ears. When the words were done, I felt energy float out of me and I felt hollow and could barely feel my feet for hours. I do not have to think or believe or have faith. I have been in the presence of the Goddess and She has been in me.

This was a wonderful experience but it happened once and time went on. I wished for the feeling the Goddess in my life again. I struggled with this. I felt Her at moments like one smells a flower scent on the air on a Spring evening. It is both undeniably there and yet elusive.

Then I was working on a meditation for a Goddess service. These usually come to me as visual images. A simple image came to me of Kwan Yin and me sipping tea watching the sunset over a calm ocean bay. There was the sweetest, gentle companionship in the moment. The scene expanded with Lakshmi, the Hindu Goddess of Prosperity, coming to sit on a pillow between us. Without me turning to look, I felt and heard the other Goddesses come and join us, receiving cups of tea from

I am the Ancient Mother. I am the source of all creation. You are my perfect, beloved Child. There is nothing in the universe I love more than you. You may have forgotten me but I have never for a moment forgotten you. You are in my arms now and for all eternity.

Message Channeled by the Author

Lakshmi, and sitting around us. I heard the soft chimes of jewelry, murmur of feminine voices greeting each other, pads of bare feet, sounds of their robes. And eventually even Kali came from the battle and laid down Her bloody weapons and cleaned up in the bay and joined us in a peaceful moment. Mary in her simple robe came and sat at our feet. We sipped tea and observed the beauty of the sunset.

All I need do is to envision this scene and I am in the presence of the Goddess again.

The Perfect, Imperfect Child

On this long journey I have learned about the Goddess as I surely expected at the outset. What I did not expect was to learn who I am. For clearly my understanding of myself has changed as I learned of Her.

With this journey I have found the Loving Mother who has never lost sight of me, who has never abandoned me, who sees every imperfection as perfectly me. My Mother knows my only name is Beloved.

I pray you can find Her, and yourself, too.

Index of Goddesses

Amaterasu, 30, 31

Ancient Mother, 5, 3, 4, 5, 8, 14, 16, 52, 67, 74, 77, 81, 107

Aphrodite, 105

Bast, 104

Bone Woman, 60-61

Bridget, 33, 57, 106

Cerridwen, 41

Crone, 19, 83

Diana, 38

Divine Feminine, 3, 17, 85, 87, 88, 99, 104

Durga, 26, 27, 104

Eagle Woman, 44

Ereshkigal, 42, 43

Flora, 24-25

Gaia, 23

Grandmother, 60, 61, 73, 83, 87

Gyhldeptis, 49

Inanna, 105

Kali, 62, 68- 69, 78, 82, 85, 96, 106, 107, 109

Kwan Yin, 20-21, 54, 76, 87, 101, 103, 109

Lakshmi, 89, 109

Maiden, 18, 38, 83

Mary, 1, 62, 78, 80, 82, 109

Mawu, 107

Mother Goddess, 1, 3, 6-7
Nu Kua, 39, 105
Oshun, 32, 104
Oya, 50, 70, 82, 87, 101, 102, 107
Pachamama, 57
Pele, 62, 82, 102, 106
Sarasvati, 46, 47, 72
Sedna, 45
Serqet, 34, 35, 87, 104
Shakti, 22
Tara, 36, 37, 62, 78, 88, 104
Tonacacihuatl, 48, 58, 59, 91
Uzume, 30, 31, 100
White Buffalo Calf Woman, 40, 106
Willendorf, 28-29

About the Author

Cynthia Lea Tootle is an ordained Interfaith Minister. She studied with the All Faiths Seminary International and currently serves as an associate minister of the Takoma Park Metaphysical Chapel.

Her ministry includes monthly services that honor the Goddess in innovative rituals that respect the traditions from which each Goddess comes and the sensibilities and needs of the modern woman. She uses her creativity to create services and classes that introduce people to many kinds of spiritual practices that open one up to intuition and spiritual energies.

She is also a Spiritual Healer and a Reiki Master.

Rev Tootle retired after 35 years working as a civilian engineer and technical manager for the US Department of Army. She has a BS in Applied Mathematics from the University of Michigan, College of Engineering and an MS in Management Science from Fairleigh Dickinson University.

Rev Tootle lives in Silver Spring, Maryland filling her spare time with gardening, Yoga, Qi Gong, and making quilts for children in need.

Made in the USA
Charleston, SC
27 September 2012